Days of the Week

Les Jours de la Semaine

French with

Max et Mathilde ™

Published by Blue Giraffe Press

Inquiries@bluegiraffepress.com

www.bluegiraffepress.com

Blue Giraffe Press Ltd. Registered office: Richmond, England

Text and illustrations @ Blue Giraffe Press Ltd 2007

Illustrated by Daryl Stevenson. Written by language consultant Carol Ellison

A catalogue record for this book is available from The British Library

Colour reproduction by Vivid • UK • www.vividprepress.com

Max et Mathilde ™

Je m'appelle:

My name is:

....

A few tips for grown-ups!

The book and CD can be used on different levels. The left-hand page introduces the child to a single word. This word is then included in a simple sentence. Stick to this if that's what you feel is most appropriate.

On the right-hand page, the dialogue delivered by Max et Mathilde introduces a slightly higher level of vocabulary and expression.

Let the pictures guide the child. A translation appears at the back of the book rather than on the page itself to avoid word-for-word translation.

Pronunciation is modelled by Max et Mathilde on the audio CD. Repetition and singing along will reinforce the vocabulary and phrases in the book.

The most important thing is to maintain the child's enthusiasm, motivation and interest in learning French. Above all, keep it simple and fun!

"Bonjour!"

Tu vas apprendre les jours de la semaine.
Tu vas t'amuser!

"Je m'appelle Max."

"Je m'appelle Mathilde."

Le chien s'appelle Noisette!

lundi

C'est lundi.

Mathilde joue du piano.

"J'aime jouer du piano!"

"Je **n'aime pas** jouer du piano!"

5

mardi

C'est mardi.

Max et Mathilde
vont à la piscine.

"Regarde-moi Mathilde!"
"Je nage comme un poisson!"

mercredi

C'est mercredi.

Max et Mathilde
jouent au tennis.

"Nous aimons jouer au tennis."

"Je gagne toujours!"

jeudi

C'est jeudi.

Max et Mathilde font
un gâteau au chocolat.

vendredi

C'est vendredi.

Max joue au football
avec son copain.

samedi

C'est samedi.

Max et Mathilde
vont pique-niquer.

"Le soleil brille." "Il fait beau!"

C'est dimanche.

Max et Mathilde
restent à la maison.

Translation and questions

Page 3

"Bonjour!" "Hello!"
Tu vas apprendre les jours de la semaine. You're going to learn the days of the week.
Tu vas t'amuser! You'll have fun!
"Je m'appelle Max." "My name is Max."
" Je m'appelle Mathilde." "My name is Mathilde."
Le chien s'appelle Noisette. The dog is called Noisette.
Ask the child their name: **"Comment t'appelles-tu?"**

4-5

lundi Monday **C'est lundi.** It's Monday.
Mathilde joue du piano. Mathilde is playing the piano.
"J'aime jouer du piano!" "I like playing the piano!"
"Je n'aime pas jouer du piano!" "I don't like playing the piano!"
Ask what the child likes doing: **"Aimes-tu jouer du piano?"**
"Aimes-tu regarder la télévision?" Encourage a response using:
"Oui, j'aime..." or **"Non, je n'aime pas..."**

6-7

mardi Tuesday **C'est mardi.** It's Tuesday.
Max et Mathilde vont à la piscine.
Max and Mathilde are going to the swimming pool.
"Regarde-moi Mathilde!" "Look at me Mathilde!"
" **Je nage comme un poisson!**" "I can swim like a fish!"
Ask if the child likes swimming: **"Aimes-tu nager?"**

8-9

mercredi Wednesday **C'est mercredi.** It's Wednesday.
Max et Mathilde jouent au tennis. Max and Mathilde are playing tennis.
"Nous aimons jouer au tennis." "We like playing tennis."
"Je gagne toujours!" " I always win!"
Ask if the child likes tennis: **"Aimes-tu jouer au tennis?"**

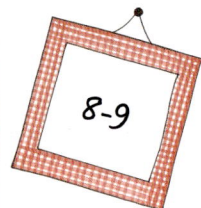

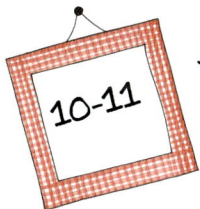

10-11 jeudi Thursday **C'est jeudi.** It's Thursday.
Max et Mathilde font un gâteau au chocolat.
Max and Mathilde are making a chocolate cake.
"Miam, miam!" "Yum, yum!"
"C'est délicieux!" "It's delicious!"
Ask if the child likes chocolate cake: **"Aimes-tu le gâteau au chocolat?"**

12-13 vendredi Friday **C'est vendredi.** It's Friday.
Max joue au football avec son copain. Max is playing football with his friend.
"Je suis champion!" "I'm the champion!"
"Non, c'est moi le champion!" "No, I'm the champion."
Ask if the child likes playing football: **"Aimes-tu jouer au football?"**

14-15 samedi Saturday **C'est samedi.** It's Saturday.
Max et Mathilde vont pique-niquer. Max and Mathilde are going on a picnic.
"Le soleil brille." "The sun is shining."
"Il fait beau!" "It's lovely weather!"
Ask if the weather is lovely today: **"Fait-il beau aujourd'hui?"**

16-17 dimanche Sunday **C'est dimanche.** It's Sunday.
Max et Mathilde restent à la maison.
Max and Mathilde are staying at home.
"Je suis très fatiguée." "I am very tired."
"Moi aussi!" "Me too!"
Ask if the child is tired: **"Es-tu fatigué(e)?"**

Now listen to Max et Mathilde on the CD as they take you
through the days of the week.
Chant out loud and sing along with them!

Les jours de la semaine

lundi
mardi
mercredi
jeudi
vendredi
samedi
dimanche

The days of the week

Monday, Tuesday, Wednesday, Thursday, Friday, Saturday, Sunday

"À bientôt!"

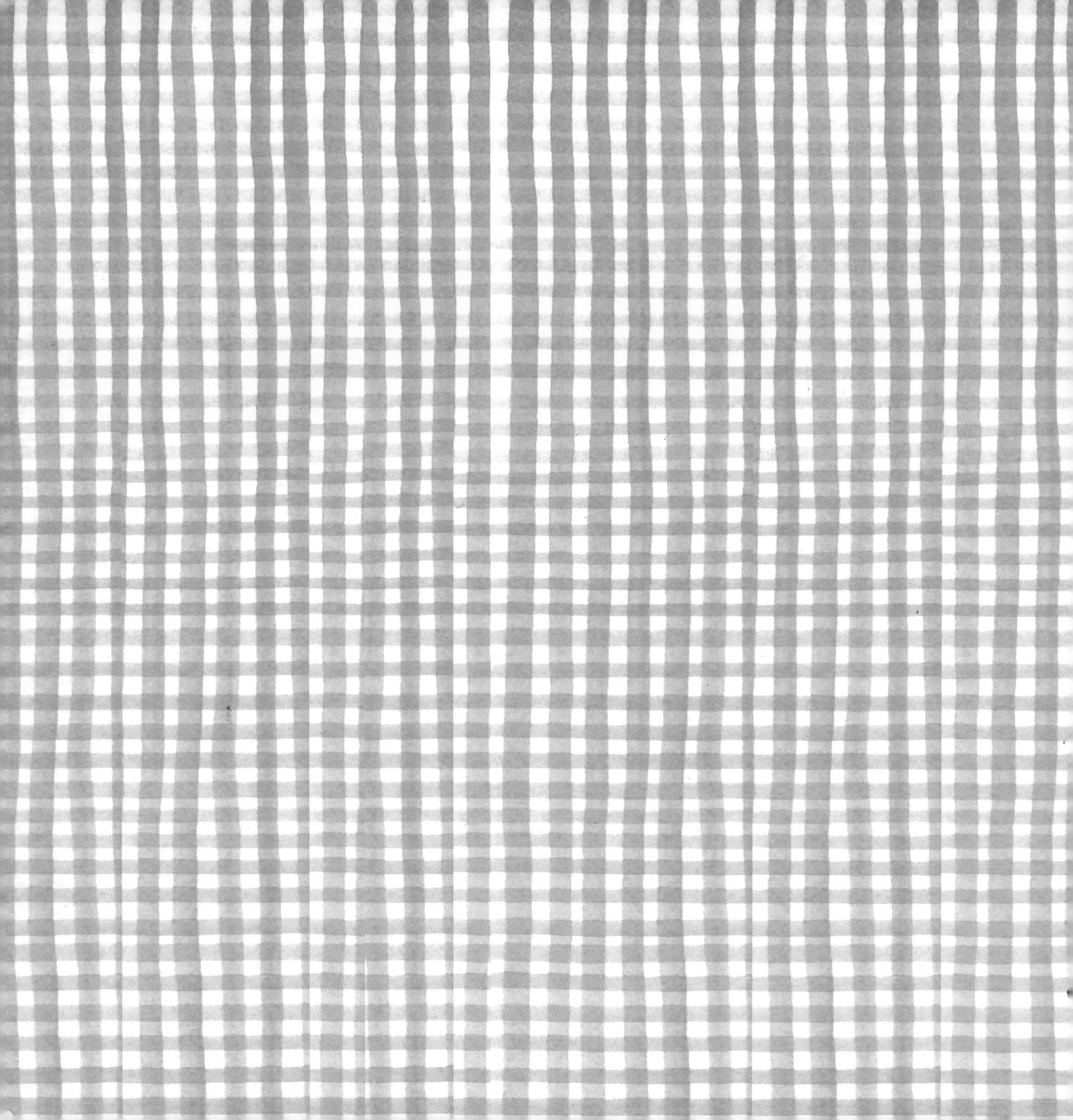